THE HOOR MAISTER'S HANDBOOK

THE HOOR MAISTER'S HANDBOOK

All the right wurds for picking up burds

SCOTT SIMPSON

BLACK & WHITE PUBLISHING

First published 2006
by Black & White Publishing Ltd
99 Giles Street, Edinburgh EH6 6BZ

ISBN 10:   1 84502 123 1
ISBN 13:   978 1 84502 123 8

British Library Cataloguing in Publication Data:
A catalogue record for this book is available
from the British Library.

Cover illustration by Scott Simpson

Printed and bound by Nørhaven Paperback A/S

CONTENTS

There are so many people to thank, so this is for everyone who helped out by supporting me, inspiring me and not taking legal action against me. Special thanks are however reserved for Shona Moir, Auld Neil, Joni Hawley and everyone at Black & White Publishing.

INGREDIENTS

This book contains the following: prejudice, ignorance, plagiarism, folklore, urban myths, wishful thinking, gross generalisation, malicious rumours, half-truths, downright lies, smut, filth, poor grammar and spelling mistakes.

THE HOOR MAISTER'S HAIKU

THE HOOR MAISTER
by R. Burns (no relation)

Boaby came tearin hame fae work, he couldnae hing
   aboot
Time fur a quick shower, a shave and a shite, then he
   wiz headin back oot.

Jumped in a fast black up the toon, met the boys in
   the Royal Mile
Says 'Ah'm only havin one mind you,' Ye see that
   wiz Boaby's style.

He didnae want tae hing aboot, in the company o'
   guys aw night
Cause aw they did wiz get steamin drunk and then
   they'd get intae a fight.

So Boaby bid a fond farewell, afore the bother started
Knocked back a pint o' fizzy pish, a nip and then
   departed.

Walked doon tae the Grassmaket, checkin each pub
that he passed
Weighin up the odds o' gettin a burd againt the odds
o' gettin glassed.

Then through the windaes o' Maggie Dicksons,
Boaby saw a wonderful sight
Twenty-eight women in matching T-shirts "Oh ya
beauty, it's a fuckin hen night."

He fought his way up tae the bar, ordered a voddie
and Red Bull
Cast a wanton yak towards the burds and wondered
which one tae pull.

There were tall ones, short ones, fat ones, thin ones,
one wiz wearin a wig
There wiz one that looked like Kylie Minogue and
another that looked like a pig.

There wiz one that looked aboot eighty-five and a
few that were underage
There wiz one wi so much body hair, she looked like
she belonged in a cage.

The bride tae be wiz a midget, nae mair than four
feet high

And she looked a bit like Gordon Brown, right doon
tae the glass eye.

She was wearin a nightgoon, had ballons in her hair
and an L-plate roond her neck
And wiz chargin guys tae gei her a kiss her, at 50
pence a peck.

In time she came to Boaby and screeched, "A kiss
fur 50p!"
To which he replied, "If ye make it a pound I'll let
ye podger me."

She laughed and said, "Ya clarty beast, a pound only
gets ye a feel."
Boaby slapped his money down on the bar and said,
"Sweetheart, you've goat a deal."

Boaby asked if he could buy her a drink, she thought
for a while and then
She said, "Ah think I'll have a bottle o' champagne,"
and Boaby said, "Think again."

The way she knocked back the voddie & Cokes
proved this lassie to be quite a drinker
But Boaby didnae mind as she fell for his patter
hook, line and fuckin sinker.

He told her to slow doon, she said, "Shut yer hole,
keep gettin in the beers."
He asked how she held her liquor and she telt him,
"By the ears."

She leaned oo'er to Boaby and gave him a big kiss on
the lips
And said, "Dae ye fancy chummin me tae get a bag
o' chips?"

It wiz on their way back from the chippy, she dragged
Boaby up a close
And when they came back he wiz sixty quid doon
and he'd caught a nasty dose.

It wiz aboot a year later he saw her again, she was
married tae Big Andy Stobie
And wiz pushin a pram wi a three-month-auld bairn
thit looks a dead ringer for Boaby.

INTRODUCTION

The idea for *The Hoor Maister's Handbook* came to me during a routine visit to the Accident & Emergency department of the Edinburgh Royal Infirmary at 11.45pm on Friday 3rd February 2006. Earlier that morning I had made the potentially fatal mistake of putting a teaspoon in the fork compartment of the cutlery drawer during my wife's menstrual cycle and she had attacked me with a bread knife. In these circumstances I usually find the best course of action is to wrap a tea towel around the wound and lock myself in the bathroom until she calms down, but on this particular occasion the blade had become lodged in my collar bone and I felt it prudent to seek immediate medical attention.

Arriving at the hospital a little after 10am I was rushed into the waiting area where I remained, drifting in and out of consciousness, for the next 13 hours before my name was called and I was transferred to the treatment area. For those of you who are unfamiliar with the average Friday night in casualty, the best way to describe the scene would be like the first twenty minutes of *Saving Private Ryan* interspersed with the last twenty minutes of *Night Of The Living Dead* with a few sectarian football songs thrown in for good measure.

In the cubicle to my right, a 22-year-old Hibernian fan was valiantly resisting the futile attempts of two nurses and a junior doctor to sew his nose back on following an incident involving a broken glass ashtray. To my left, a 35-year-old Rangers fan with a size eleven bootprint on his forehead and a fractured skull was angrily comparing the no smoking policy of the hospital to living in Nazi Germany. No sooner had he been taken away for X-Rays than his place was taken by an unconscious 19-year-old Hearts fan who was handcuffed to a policeman. Later on he would be charged with attempted murder.

It could have been that I was in a particularly nostalgic mood and was viewing the past through rose-tinted glasses, although a far more likely reason might have been the morphine, but I found myself harking back to a far more civilised time. To a time before alcopops and two-for-the-price-of-one promotions. To a time before Stanley knives and claw hammers were considered fashion accessories. To a time when the only thing on a young man's mind on Friday night was getting his Nat King Cole.

Friday night was the night when the young single

guys of Scotland would pull on their lucky underpants, splash a couple of handfuls of Blue Stratos aftershave under their oxters and, with a week's wages tucked into their back pockets, they would seek out gullible and easily impressed women with all the skill and dedication of a big game hunter tracking lions in the jungles of Africa. And no-one was more determined than the hoor maisters. The hoor maisters knew just where to look and just what to look for. They were fluent in bullshit, they collected names and phone numbers in the same obsessive way a trainspotter might collect the numbers of steam locomotives. Most importantly, the hoor maister realises that when it comes to the opposite sex there is no such thing as an ugly woman, just fussy guys.

But what is a hoor maister? Well, a literal translation of the Scots dialect from which it is derived would be "whore master" although this is something of a misnomer as hoor maisters are by no means pimps.

They might perhaps be described as philanderers, but a far more accurate description would be a male whore. These low-income lotharios have existed since prehistoric times in Scotland. In fact it's well known that the Picts did so much shagging that it became impractical to wear clothes and they simply took to painting themselves blue. When Christianity arrived in Scotland, it was hoped that the natives would consent to wearing trousers and, following a couple of hundred years of negotiations, a compromise was reached when the Scots agreed to wear kilts on the understanding that they didn't have to bother with underpants. This did little to stem the increase in ginger babies being born.

Despite the attempts of Calvinism and strict Presbyterian churches, hoor maisters continued to flourish in Scotland right up until the outbreak of the First World War when hundreds of thousands of Scots signed up to fight for King and Country. No sooner had the brave men sailed across the English Channel to do battle with the vile Hun, than the hoor maisters emerged from their hiding places to a country in which women out-numbered men by approximately 350 to 1.

As was to be expected, there were the inevitable casualties of war and by 1917 it was estimated that as many as 400 men a week were succumbing to venereal disease in Scotland. By the end of the war hoor maister numbers had fallen to an all time low but it was thanks to another Scot, Sir Alexander Fleming, who discovered penicillin, that the hoor maister was saved from extinction.

The 1960s and 70s were halcyon days for the hoor maister. The advent of flower power and free love signalled an end to the stigma of sex outwith the confines of marriage (with the exception of the Western Isles where it is still punishable by burning at the stake) and casual sex was as much a part of Friday night as McEwans Export and white pudding suppers. Of course, there was always the odd act of random violence but given the choice of a knee-trembler with a young lady in a shop doorway or kicking seven shades of shite out of a complete stranger, most guys went for the first option.

Then along came the 1980s and with it came AIDS. Acquired Immune Deficiency Syndrome wasn't something that could be cured with a quick visit to the S.T.D. clinic for a wee jag in the arse. This was a killer and the days of casual sex and one-night stands were well and truly at an end.

Things got so bad that women were demanding written references and a full medical history before allowing a guy to buy them a drink. This in turn meant that pubs and clubs were full to bursting with hordes of young males, hornier than a Viking hat shop and fuelled by a volatile mixture of alcohol and testosterone.

Now that women were no longer interested in them they turned their sights on each other and, not wishing to be thought of as homosexuals, they proceeded to batter each other's melt in. And so it has continued now for more than twenty years.

And this brings us back to the Accident & Emergency department of the Edinburgh Royal Infirmary. As I was having eight inches of Sheffield steel removed from my neck, I got to thinking of ways in which I could help my fellow man and put an end to the senseless violence which has turned Friday nights in the city centres of Scotland into a bloodbath.

Following quite literally four or five hours of extensive research, I have compiled this handbook in an attempt to persuade the young guys of Scotland to channel their energies into something a little more positive than kicking someone to death outside a chip shop simply because they looked at you in the wrong way. Of course, there are far more productive alternatives, such as joining a gym and getting fit or helping out with some charitable organisation, but that's nowhere near as much fun as scuttling a young lady from behind in a pub car park.

By following the clear and concise instructions in *The Hoor Maister's Handbook* you will soon learn exactly which types of girls to go for, where to find them, what to tell them, what to do to them and how to do it all over again the following week with someone else.

Now go and fill yer boots . . .

Burds that are best avoided

1

TYPES OF WOMEN

Scotland has a population of just over 5.1 million with females accounting for approximately 52% of the country. This gives us somewhere in the region of 2,652,000 women. Of course we can immediately discount those above and below a certain age and those women who bat for the other side. Here's a handy mnemonic you may find helpful when it comes to narrowing your search: S.O.Y. In times past it used to be S.O.Y.A., with the A standing for available, but if history has taught the hoor maister anything, it's that it takes more than a ring on a lassie's finger to keep his tadger in his trolleys.

The S stands for straight, so first ask yourself, is she straight? Times have changed since the 1980s when lesbians were easily identified by their shaved heads, donkey jackets, comfortable shoes and faces like bulldogs licking piss off a nettle. Modern lesbians are virtually indistinguishable from other females and, as is often the case, a hefty boot in the bollocks is sometimes required to convince the more persistent hoor maister of a young lady's preferred sexual orientation.

The O stands for old enough, so ask yourself, is she old enough? Then ask yourself again, is she old enough? This is by far the most important criteria and cannot be emphasised enough. Although 16 years is the legal age of consent in Scotland, the prudent hoor maister will avoid females who appear younger than 19 for fear of having their names put on a special list and being sent to prison where fellow inmates will piss in their food.

The Y stands for young enough, so is she young enough? This is by no means as important as the previous criteria but it's important to set yourself a limit and try to stick to it. Should you find yourself escorting a slightly more mature female back to her place and find you have to slow down so she can keep up with you without getting breathless, you may want to seriously consider lowering your threshold by ten years or so. So for argument's sake, let's set the ceiling at 40 years of age.

According to figures plucked entirely out of thin air, there are just over 69,000 heterosexual women between 19 and 40 years of age currently residing in Scotland and, to the untrained eye, they fall into two basic categories. Stoaters (blonde hair, long legs, hourglass figure, tits like space hoppers) and Morts (overweight, face like a blind cobbler's thumb, tits like a cocker spaniel's ears). The hoor maister, however, has a 10-point descending scale by which females are graded according to their physical appearance and will only concern himself with females between 7 and 4, with 3 as an emergency reserve.

10

Perfect 10s are still extremely rare in Scotland and those that do exist often have their potential recognised at birth and are taken out of the country before the harsh climate and abysmal dietary habits can inflict any further harm to their skin, hair and waistlines. The last authentically recorded perfect 10 in Scotland was the supermodel Kirsty Hume who was born in Ayrshire in 1976 and now lives in Los Angeles.

9

Just because they'll never make the cover of *Cosmopolitan*, 9s are still drop-dead gorgeous and certainly wouldn't look out of place in the line-up of an all-girl pop group where the ability to look good in a pair of hot pants and a boob tube far outweighs a painfully obvious lack of talent. Unless you play centre forward for a premier league football team, you have absolutely no chance whatsoever.

8

Still gorgeous enough to grace the pages of certain magazines found on the top shelf of your local newsagent or dancing around a pole in lap dancing bar, yet all the while remaining safely out of the league of even the most optimistic hoor maister.

7

It's only at this point that the hoor maister has any real chance of scoring and it's only in certain circumstances that a young lady of this calibre might consent to allowing you within ten feet of her. Perhaps she has an ex-boyfriend whom she wants to make jealous. Perhaps she is trapped in a downward spiral of self-loathing and needs to affirm her own worthlessness or perhaps it's just morbid curiosity. Whatever the case, you might want to finish your drinks quickly and get back to her place before she comes to her senses and sees you for what you really are.

6 & 5

These borderline boilers have in recent years come to be known as BOBFOCs, an acronym which stands for Body Of *Baywatch*, Face Of *Crimewatch*. In many cases it would take nothing more than a Remington lady shave to elevate this particular female to a 7 or a couple of fish suppers to send her down to a 4.

4

A bit fat.

3

Often referred to as Sengas, they are easily identified by their orange faces, an effect they achieve by substituting Ronseal wood stain for make-up. These trolls are more used to breaking legs than breaking hearts and should only ever be used as a last resort for the hoormaister. They have a great deal in common with the praying mantis and, following an all too disappointing sexual encounter, they are likely to bite your fucking head off.

2

This is, in all probability, the last level at which they can still be positively identified as females without an accompanying letter from a doctor.

1

Almost as rare as the perfect 10, the unfortunate

females who occupy this end of the scale were, until recent years, confined to a remote island 72 miles off the north-west coast of Scotland and were the results of biological warfare experiments carried out by the MOD. Many of those who managed to escape the island and swim ashore were rounded up and mistakenly confined to zoos, although a few made it as far as Glasgow and were given leading roles in the BBC Scotland soap opera *River City*.

2

WHERE TO FIND WOMEN

The Street

Great for watching the girls go by; especially on those all too rare days when the sun comes out to play and the ladies shed three or four layers of wool. But, when it comes to actually making contact with the opposite sex, the high street is far from ideal.

You've probably seen that well known television commercial for a certain brand of body spray in which a young guy walking down the street gets a whiff of perfume from a stunningly attractive young lady walking in the opposite direction. Off he goes in search of a bunch of flowers and upon handing them over he is rewarded with a coy smile which seems to suggest that her knickers are in her handbag.

The very same scenario acted out in Sauchiehall Street would almost certainly culminate in a pair of severely swollen testicles and a restraining order. So, unless you bear a striking resemblance to Brad Pitt

When a guy suddenly gives a woman flowers
he's taking his life in his hands

in both physical and financial terms, I'd give the high street a miss if I were you.

At Work

Workplace liaisons almost always spell disaster and should be avoided at all costs. Less experienced hoor maisters have made the mistake of making a move on their female bosses and, following an all too disappointing podger in the stationery cupboard, found themselves the recipient of every shitty job that comes along. Worse still, the hoor maister that gets the office junior drunk in order to cop a quick feel during the Christmas party may very well find himself in front of an industrial tribunal.

Church

It might seem an odd choice of venue but churches can offer so much more than salvation of the soul. First of all, the women who attend church take a great deal of pride in their appearance. They also have the added bonus of being a bit on the gullible side. Let's face it – a woman who takes the good book at face value might not be so quick to doubt your claims of being a stuntman with a house in the south of France. Another great thing about Christian girls is that even if they do reject your advances they often find more diplomatic ways to do so rather than kicking you in the bollocks and calling you a clatty bastard.

Weddings

There's nothing like a good old-fashioned wedding reception to loosen the elastic on a lady's knickers. From the bride's mother who's had a couple of sherries too many and is in a highly suggestible state of mind to the bridesmaids who are bitterly resentful of the fact it's not their big day and subliminally need to be reassured. Remember, though, that should you find yourself baw-deep with the girl in the white dress at a wedding the chances are you've either taken a dreadful liberty or, worse still, you're the silly bastard that just got hitched.

Funerals

Okay, so it may be a little bit beyond the pale to go on the pull while some poor bugger is being planted but, on the plus side, women look sexy in black. A bereavement and a few bevvies often lead women to do things they wouldn't normally do and, when they sober up, the burden of guilt is on them.

The Supermarket

As odd as it may seem, supermarkets can be fantastic places for meeting single women. So much so that some of the larger chains have gone as far as to introduce singles evenings. One of the best things about supermarkets is that you can tell a lot about a woman simply by observing the contents of her shopping basket. So the next time you're strolling around Lidl's and you spot a woman on the wrong side of forty who is carrying a shopping basket containing a frozen meal for one, a giant Toblerone and a forty ounce bottle of Bacardi, why not introduce yourself?

Lonely Hearts Columns

It's highly unlikely that you'll encounter anything higher on the scale than a four in the personal columns of your local newspaper, despite the flattering descriptions they like to attribute to themselves.

The trick is to understand that, when a woman describes herself as decisive in a personal ad, what she really means is that she's a stroppy cow who likes to get her own way. Here are a few more common descriptive terms found in the average lonely hearts

'Aw, shit!'

columns and the terms you can safely substitute:

athletic	*flat chested*
attentive	*jealous*
cuddly	*fat*
curvaceous	*morbidly obese*
homely	*desperate*
liberated	*hairy*
rugged	*ugly*
sensual	*expensive*
shy	*sullen*
sophisticated	*snobbish*
warm	*possessive*
witty	*loud*

Bingo

Bingo halls have undergone dramatic changes in the last few years. No longer the haunts of octogenarian coffin dodgers, the sweet smell of lavender masking the stale stench of urine has long since been blown away, as women, some as young as their early forties, have been lured by the promise of a great night out and the chance to win as much as £5,000,000. The novice hoor maister who finds himself surrounded by three or four hundred women in a bingo hall may very well think he's died and gone to heaven. But should he make the mistake of trying to chat up a bingo bint during the link-up game that's just what might happen. These women are there to play bingo and the only guy they have eyes for is the gormless-looking bugger calling out the numbers, so unless you want to spend the remainder of the evening having a magic marker surgically removed from your eye socket I'd give the bingo a wide berth.

Lap Dancing Bars

Don't be so fucking stupid.

Pubs and Clubs

The preferred venue for hoor maisters the world over. Pubs and clubs offer a relaxed atmosphere, the right kind of ambience and, more importantly, the copious amounts of the alcohol required to persuade young ladies to fall for your charms.

Taxi Ranks

You don't have to be wearing an Armani suit or be hung like a Clydesdale horse when you're standing at the front of a long queue at a taxi rank. There's just always been something about this kind of guy that women find attractive. So, if you still haven't scored by the end of the night and you find yourself about to hop in a taxi and head home, take a look at who else is in the queue. If you should happen to spy a wobbly young woman, kebab in one hand and a dreadfully uncomfortable pair of shoes in the other, ask where she is going. No matter if it's five minutes down the road or the other side of the fucking country, it's on your way and you'd be more than happy to drop her off. It's not until the taxi is in motion that you explain to her that you have lost your keys and you're going to have to spend the next three or four hours standing outside your front door waiting for a locksmith to arrive. Play your cards right and she might just show her gratitude by asking you in for a coffee. On the other hand she could just as well say, "Tough titty ya muppet!" and you get stuck with the fare from her gaff back to yours.

The Pavement Outside Pubs and Clubs

A whole new venue for picking up women came into play on Sunday, March 26, 2006 when the Scottish Executive outlawed smoking in bars. Now every time a female smoker wants to light up she is forced to venture outside where she can fully expect to be greeted by a horde of eager hoor maisters. In what has quickly come to be known as "smirting" (a cross between smoking and flirting), hoor maisters, even non-smoking hoor maisters, have taken up residence outside the pubs and clubs of Scotland where they eagerly await weak-willed ladies to whom they can offer a light, shelter from the rain (many hoor maisters have taken to carrying umbrellas for this very purpose) and a sympathetic ear.

"Yes, it is a dreadful violation of our civil liberties isn't it? Can I buy you a drink?"

"The victim is believed to be a twenty-four-year-old female with blonde hair and big tits. It appears that she stepped outside for a cigarette and twenty-eight hoor maisters offered her a light at the same time."

3

BE PREPARED

You wouldn't expect a fireman to enter a burning building without protective clothing, breathing apparatus and an axe, would you? Nor would you expect a taxi driver to get behind the wheel of his cab without a big fat arse, an overpowering stench of body odour and an opinion on every fucking subject under the sun. Before venturing out for an evening on the pull the hoor maister will spend up to fifteen minutes preparing himself for a number of eventualities and will both dress and equip himself accordingly.

Underpants
Unless you're the proud owner of a pair of brilliant white designer underpants, it's best to go commando. Nothing, but nothing, kills the mood faster than a pair of off-white, threadbare shreddies emblazoned with a cartoon worm on a hook and the words "Girl Bait".

Similarly, unless you have the well-toned body of a Greek god, that leopard skin posing pouch is doing you no favours whatsoever.

Shirt

Despite the fact that even during the height of summer temperatures in Scotland rarely climb higher than four below zero, the only acceptable item of clothing to be worn on a night out is a good quality short-sleeved shirt. The wearing of a coat often leads to accusations of flagrant homosexuality.

Jeans

In days gone by many nightclubs had a strict dress code and enforced a zero tolerance approach to jeans. Times have changed and jeans have become perfectly acceptable at even the most exclusive establishments. At the time of writing it's fashionable to wear jeans which are at least eight sizes too big for you, look as though they have been involved in a serious road traffic accident and cost upwards of £160.

Socks

First and foremost, unless you're a bus driver or a postman, you have no excuse for wearing white terry towelling socks. Don't do it. It's as simple as that.

Most hoor maisters wear two pairs of socks when going out on the pull. The first pair is traditionally worn on your feet and should on no account ever be taken off (see below), while the second pair (ideally a pair of heavy football socks) is stuffed down the front of your trousers to impress women. This serves the dual purpose of making you look unfeasibly well endowed while at the same time offering a certain amount of protection to the genitals from ladies who fail to find your somewhat direct approach remotely amusing.

Shoes

Like jeans, the wearing of trainers in nightclubs is no longer grounds for the door men to drag you around the corner and kick your head in. But, whether you wear shoes or trainers, it's a good idea to opt for the slip-on or Velcro-strap variety as opposed to lace-ups. Should you find yourself lucky enough to be invited back to her place at the end of the evening and have to make a quick escape (kids asking if you are their new daddy or husband coming home earlier than anticipated) you don't want to waste valuable seconds having to lace up a pair of 24-inch Dr Martens.

There are various other items of equipment that the well prepared hoor maister should get into the habit of carrying whilst on the pull.

Money

For obvious reasons, the bulk of your money should be stashed safely in your right sock. It's a sad reflection on the society we live in but in Scotland you are five times more likely to be robbed by a pretty young lady than a knife-wielding heroin addict. The only difference is that it takes a little longer to realise you've been mugged. So the next time you're having your arse groped by a girl in a shop doorway, ask yourself, "Is she just being friendly or am I being mugged?"

A good tip is to carry a wallet stuffed with pieces of newspaper cut to the same size as £20 notes. The bulge in your wallet will serve to impress the average female far more than the bulge caused by the football socks down the front of your pants and every time you pay a visit to the toilet you can transfer a couple of quid from your sock to the wallet.

Here's another handy tip that'll have the girls frothing at the gash. Keep about fifty pence in loose change (five, two and one pence pieces) in your pocket and when you pass one of the hundreds of beggars which congregate in city centres on a Friday night, dip into your pocket and pull out a large handful of coins, hand it to the beggar and say, "Go and get yourself a hot meal my friend."

The female now stupidly thinks that you're a generous and caring human being and the chances of you getting inside her knickers have just doubled.

Lighter

Even if you're a non-smoker, you should get into the habit of carrying a cigarette lighter with you at all times. Ever since the smoking ban came into effect, the pavements outside pubs and clubs are literally heaving with weak-willed females and you should be on hand to offer them a light as soon as that ciggie is in their lips. It's worth investing in a good quality petrol lighter for this very purpose, as the cheaper disposable lighters are often unreliable and, what's more, they make you look like a pikey.

Handkerchief

Another optional extra, which comes in handy when dealing with the inevitable blubbering female who's had a few too many and is now getting slightly emotional. Simply offer her your handkerchief, a few reassuring words and watch her knickers fly across the room.

Pen and Paper

How many times have you asked for a girl's telephone number only to suffer the embarrassment of frantically searching for a pen and a beer mat to write it on? More often than not you are forced to carve the number into the back of a cigarette packet with a spent match. A great tip is to carry a small pen or pencil (the ones that betting shops supply are ideal for this very purpose) with a small sheet of paper wrapped around it. This can be kept in your back pocket or, if you smoke, it can sit inside your cigarette packet.

Mints

Following 14 pints of lager, 40 high-tar ciggies and a tortoise vindaloo, your breath will probably start to smell like the rotting corpse of a farmyard animal. So unless you're one of those sexual deviants who get turned on by women vomiting in their face, you might want to keep a packet of Polos on standby.

Condoms

This is by far the most important item in the hoor maister's kit and its importance cannot be emphasised enough. Do not leave home without one, or, if you're feeling particularly lucky, two or three. Not only do condoms help prevent all manners of sexually transmitted diseases, they can help to prevent certain government agencies from hunting you down like a dog and removing 75% of your annual income from your bank account.

4

MAKING A MOVE

BODY LANGUAGE

Now that we know the type of girl to look out for and where to find them, the next step is to ascertain whether or not they want anything to do with you. Despite almost fifty years of female emancipation, Scottish women are essentially old-fashioned creatures who still expect a fella to make the first move, and you're likely to be in for one hell of a long wait should you be foolish enough to expect otherwise.

Of course, it's not outwith the bounds of common decency to simply approach the first woman that happens to take your fancy, offer to buy her a drink and hope that she drags you back to her place to indulge in prolonged acts of unspeakable sexual depravity. Unfortunately, this somewhat direct approach all too often runs the very real risk of being told to go away and take a flying fuck at one's self.

Thankfully, there are a number of subtle signs

"I think she likes me."

women send out which, if read correctly, can mean the difference between a sure thing and a smack in the pus.

Colour plays an important part in defining a female's personality. Women who wear yellow are often confident and outgoing, whereas women who dress in blue are often a little more down to earth and can be prone to shyness. Red, as you might expect, signifies an adventurous nature with a slight taste for danger, and women who dress in black are usually fat.

Then there are the physical signs that women subconsciously send out. Body language is nature's way of saving the hoor maister a lot of time, effort and the price of a Bacardi breezer but, be warned – just as the spoken language in Scotland is vastly different to that spoken in the rest of the United Kingdom, the same must be said for body language. A girl in Ipswich could be sending out subliminal messages that she is interested in a guy by tugging on the sleeves of her blouse. Whereas a girl doing the same thing in Greenock could just as easily be trying to conceal a home-made tattoo which reads 'All Coppers Are Bastards'.

Here are a few more tips that should enable the most illiterate of hoor maisters to read women like a book.

Posture

You can tell an awful lot about a woman simply by observing the way she sits at a table. A girl who doesn't wish to be bothered will create an invisible barrier around herself by sitting as far forward in her chair as she can. She will also have her legs crossed, arms folded in front of her and a look on her face which quite clearly says, "Fuck off or I'll stab you in the face."

Of course the exact opposite of this frosty female would be a woman slumped back in her chair, legs wide open, arms hanging loosely by her side and a far-away look in her eyes. Tempting as this may sound, she is quite clearly pissed out of her skull and has lapsed into unconsciousness. Any attempt made on a girl in this advanced state of intoxication would quite rightly lead to criminal proceedings and your name would be placed on the sex offenders' register. Anything in between these two examples is fair game.

The Eyes

The eyes have been described as the windows to the soul but beware, as in run-down areas the windows are often boarded up.

Once you have your sights set on a girl, you should stare directly at her until she notices you. You may want to spend a little time at home in front of a mirror practicing your staring technique until you have mastered a gaze which suggests a genuine interest in getting to know her better as opposed to looking for a fight.

Scottish women are by no means as fragile as their southern counterparts so, if she asks you to step outside for a square go, you may want to put a little more practice into your technique or take judo lessons. Assuming your staring technique is up to speed and she notices you, you should respond by raising an eyebrow and flashing a suave smile. Should the smile be reciprocated you should move like shit off a shovel and offer to buy her a drink.

Hair

Women place a great deal of importance in their hair, and paying attention to the way she constantly seems to be fiddling with it can help to discover just what's on her mind.

If she is moving her hair away from her face then it means she wants to be noticed whereas a woman pulling her fringe down means she is shy. If a girl is looking at you and twirling the ends of her hair around her fingers this means she really likes you. Should the girl have a tendency to drag her fingernails through her scalp she most probably has head lice and you should seriously think about raising your standards.

Hands

The first thing to look for when observing a woman's hands is that tell-tale white band of flesh on the ring finger of her left hand which indicates that her husband thinks she's at the bingo with her sister.

Now take a look at her fingernails. There's nothing sexier than long, elaborately painted fingernails, but ask yourself this question – do you really want three-inch razor-sharp talons anywhere near your tackle? Ideally you should be looking for women who have chewed their fingernails down to the quick, worried in case their husbands find out that they aren't at the bingo with their sister. Big hands usually indicate that she's actually a bloke.

Feet

For some strange and inexplicable reason women tend to point their feet towards men they would like to get to know a little better. It is, however, worth noting that they do the exact same thing just before they kick you in the plums, so it's a theory you may not wish to invest too much faith in.

5

BEER GOGGLES

We've all heard of beer goggles – that mysterious condition in which the physical appearance of women alters in accordance with the amount of alcohol you ingest. Of course, beer goggles do not as yet exist in any physical form, which is regrettable, as it would make watching *River City* a far less harrowing experience. Now let's take a look at the more beneficial effects of consuming ridiculous amounts of fizzy falling down juice.

Look at these venomous harridans. They look as though they have fallen from the ugly tree and hit every single branch on the way down. No man in his right mind would give them as much as a second glance, but the night is still young.

As you can see, there has been quite a transformation. As the alcohol travels through the bloodstream it switches off the parts of the brain which deal with physical repellence, and minor imperfections in the female form drift away, allowing their inner beauty to shine through. Except, of course, for the girl on the far right, who is ugly to the bone. In order to make this poor lassie look vaguely attractive you would have to knock back somewhere in the region of 24 pints, a couple of bottles of cooking sherry and a certain amount of illegal drugs. This would however have a knock-on effect on everyone else . . .

Enough said.

6

CHAT UP LINES

The year was 1314 and, on the night before the great battle of Bannockburn, Robert the Bruce and his brave knights had gathered in the great hall of some castle or other to eat, drink and be merry, for in the morning they might die. At some point in the evening's proceedings the king approached a 22-year-old serving wench named Daphne McCafferty and said, "Such is thy beauty, that if I saw thee naked I would die a happy man." Daphne said to the king in return, "Aye, and if I saw you naked I'd probably die laughing. Now beat it, ya numpty!"

Humiliated, the king ran from the castle and hid in a cave. It was here that Robert the Bruce saw a spider trying to build a web and it was this very spider that inspired the king to reflect, "If at first you don't succeed, try, try again." This prompted him to return to the castle where he cheerfully slapped the arse of Jenny Dowell, a 45-year-old seamstress and said, "Awright doll, gonnae get yer jaws aroond mah baws?" The rest, as they say, is history.

If the last 700 years have taught us anything, it's that chat-up lines require a certain amount of perseverance and that Daphne McCafferty was probably a lesbian anyway.

Here is a brief selection of chat-up lines which are unlikely to result in more than a beamer and a smack in the pus but you'll never know unless you give them a go.

"Do you know the difference between my nob and a scotch egg? No? Well how would you like to go on a picnic with me?"

"Do you sleep on your stomach? No? Can I?"

"Do you fancy a fuck and a fish supper? No? Why – do you not like fish?"

"Do you fancy going halves on a bastard?"

"Do you fancy a shag? No? Well, would you mind lying still while I have one?"

"If it's true that we are what we eat, I could be you by tomorrow morning."

"Let's go back to your place and do the things I'm going to tell my pals we did anyway."

"The only reason I'd kick you out of bed would be to shag you on the floor."

"If I said you had a beautiful body would you let me cum on your tits?"

"If I told you I had a tiny nob would you let me shag you? No? Good 'cause it's fucking massive."

"It's not going to suck itself you know."

"Can you suck your own tits? No? Can I?"

Alternatively you might like to borrow a line from the great Scottish bard and celebrated hoor maister Rabbie Burns himself.

"Roses are red, violets are blue,
I'd like to tear the hole off of you."

7

BUYING A DRINK

If you've got this far and don't as yet have a sharp throbbing pain in the testicles you might like to think about buying the young lady in question a drink. This is another fantastic opportunity to ascertain how the rest of the evening is likely to pan out. If she asks for a Coke, then it's a clear sign that she doesn't trust you and wants to keep her wits about her. Don't be disheartened by her suspicious nature, just slip a treble vodka into her soft drink and hope she doesn't notice. It's then only a matter of time before she lets her guard and, with a little patience, her knickers down.

Here are a few other tipples and the secrets they reveal:

Water	She's probably a bible basher
Aftershock	She's a nutter

Bacardi Breezer	She isn't wearing any underwear
Champagne	She's taking the piss
Snakebite	She's underage
Super Lager	She's an alcoholic
80 Shilling	She's a fee spirited individual who doesn't believe in pre-conceived ideas concerning sexuality. Still, just to be on the safe side, it's best to check the size of her hands and look for signs of an Adam's apple.

8

LIES

It has been said that a successful relationship is built on a strong foundation of trust and honesty. One-night stands, on the other hand, are built entirely on deceit. From little white lies such as, "Oh, that's interesting, do tell me more," and, "I'd say you were no older than your mid-twenties," to great big stinking black fibs like, "Honest, I won't cum in your mouth," and, "Don't worry, I've had the snip anyway."

At this early stage, however, all the lies you tell should be in a vain effort to make yourself appear far more interesting than you really are. You may decide to go completely overboard by telling her that you earn thousands of pounds a month as a stuntman, airline pilot or some other fantastically impressive occupation. You could, however, simply exaggerate the importance of your own career. If, for example, you earn a living wiping the arses of coffin dodgers in some old folks' home, you might prefer to dress it up a little by telling her that you are a posterior hygienist in the care sector.

There are a number of shitty, dead-end, soul-destroying jobs that can be glamorised with a certain amount of creative truth bending. For instance, a produce replenishment technician sounds a damn sight more interesting than a shelf stacker in Scotmid, and a domicile relocation agent sounds as though he earns a lot more money than a furniture removals man.

On a more precautionary note, you should at some point in the evening slip the fact that you have an identical twin brother into the conversation. This seemingly meaningless fib might just pay off when you bump into her nine months later as she is pushing a pram down the street. It's at this point that you can break the sad news of your own death.

9

"YOUR PLACE OR MINE?"

Okay, so it's a cliché, but it's a point that has to be addressed at some point in the evening's proceedings. Whenever humanly possible you should strive to ensure that it's her place as opposed to yours. Apart from the obvious inconvenience of having to get rid of her the following morning, you might be in danger of shattering the slightly more glamorous illusions you spent all evening building around yourself when she discovers a sink full of dirty dishes and your wardrobe groaning under the weight of your vast Grumble magazine collection. You should even go so far as to tell outrageous lies in an effort to dissuade her, such as: "I would invite you back to my place but it burned down this morning and the firemen are still there trying to put it out," or, "Sorry babes, but I just sold it and I still haven't got around to buying a new one yet."

If you're feeling flush you might consider shelling out a couple of quid on a hotel room. Night porters in certain hotels have been known to offer the use of a room for an hour or so in exchange for a crisp ten pound note on the strict understanding that you make the bed when you've finished and stay the hell out of the mini bar.

If you're having difficulty in finding a dishonest night porter (although this is highly unlikely) or you haven't got a tenner to spare, those helpful chappies at the town planning offices have provided a number of locations which, over the years, have proved to be adequately suitable for a quick knee-trembler. Stairwells, car parks, shop doorways, bus shelters and telephone boxes offer a small modicum of privacy and are all ideal places for a spot of al fresco copulation. Don't be put off by CCTV cameras either – the guys back in the control room are unlikely to alert the authorities until they have caught the entire act on videotape and made a few copies to show their mates.

Another great place to get familiar with the ladies is in the back of a taxi. Taxi drivers are among the most morally reprehensible creatures on the face of the planet and have been known to turn the meter off and take the long way home so they can better observe the goings-on in their rear view mirrors.

10

THE McKAMA SUTRA

Ask the average Scotsman if he's ever heard of the *Kama Sutra* and he's likely to say yes, but he finds it a bit too spicy and prefers the chicken tikka masala instead.

There is another book, however, which makes the world's most famous sex manual look like a late Victorian copy of *The People's Friend*. *The McKama Sutra* was written by Archie McKama, a footman in the service of Lord Donald McCathie, the 11th Earl of Gracemount. The sexual exploits of Lord McCathie were legendary and between the years 1819 and 1834 it has been estimated that he pumped some 5,500 women and sired over 19,000 illegitimate children before his bollocks withered to the size of sultanas and fell off. To this day his descendants account for more than 23% of Scotland's population.

It was young Archie's job to remain outside the earl's bedchamber, keep a watchful eye out for Lady McCathie and then smuggle female guests out of the castle in the early hours of the morning. Boredom and curiosity eventually got the better of the footman and he took to climbing down the chimney and hanging upside down by his feet in the fireplace to observe the insatiable and often bizarre antics of his master. Back in his room, Archie would make notes and illustrations which he collected over a number of years.

Following the demise of the Earl in 1834, Archie McKama travelled to Edinburgh with his notes in search of a publisher and, after four long years of rejection, the book was eventually published by Dobbie's of Leith, an up-and-coming publishing house which specialised in left-handed literature. Bearing in mind that attitudes towards sex were slightly more conservative than today, there was something of an outcry and, following a brief trial on September 19th, 1839, the jury brought back a guilty verdict and both Archie McKama and Deek Dobbie were taken to what is now the foot of Leith Walk and hanged by the neck until dead.

Almost every copy of the book was burned and now the only copy which is on public display is in the National Museum of Scotland at Chambers Street, Edinburgh. It's rolled up and stuffed behind the cistern of the third cubicle in the gents' toilets. Please remember to put it back when you're finished and also remember to wash your hands.

Due to guidelines carefully laid down in the Obscene Publications Acts of 1959 and 1964, we are unable to reproduce some of the more exotic positions illustrated in the original book. In fact, even describing what takes place in the "Tam O' Shanter", "Jaggy Thistle" or "Bagpiper's Elbow" could lead to a fine of up to £500,000 and 6 years in prison.

Here are a few examples of what we thought we might get away with . . .

STIRRING THE PORRIDGE

Also known as haggis bashing, this is by far the most popular sexual act performed by Scottish males as it involves the bare minimum of effort and there is no need to buy your right hand eight bottles of Bacardi Breezer to get it in the mood or phone it a taxi home once the deed has been done.

Here's a handy tip for maximising your pleasure – just before you start, lie on your right arm until it goes to sleep and it feels as though someone else is whacking you off. Make sure you get this the right way around, as lying on your nob until it goes to sleep makes it feel as though you're doing it to someone else and completely defeats the purpose.

THE 68

Popular at weddings and other occasions at which highland dress is worn, this is a Caledonian variation of the 69 position. In this case it is the male who receives all the benefits and assures his companion that he owes her one.

THE SALTIRE

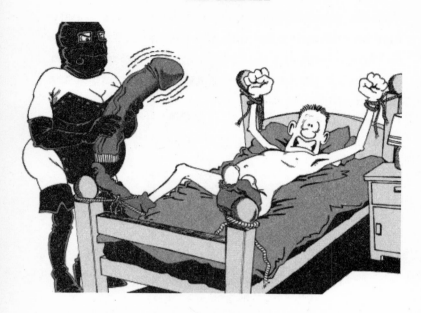

One for the more sexually adventurous but, be warned, this position can leave you in a state of vulnerability.

THE LOCH NESS MONSTER

As it's name suggests, this particular act of depravity may be nothing more than an urban myth. Not only because of the extreme physical demands it makes on those concerned but also because it's highly unlikely that you'll ever find anyone willing to participate.

To begin with you will need a ██████ ██████████, a

█████, two █████████ and a ████████ which you can buy from your local butcher's shop. You might find it useful to keep a couple of ███████ on standby just in case the ████████ becomes lodged in your ████████. You start by taking a firm grip of your partner's ████████ and get into a position in which your ████████ is just between her ███████ and ██████████. You can then move your ███████ in and out of her ████████ without your █████████ getting tangled in her ████████. You should then take hold of the █████████, ███████████ and one of the █████████ and insert them into your own █████████.

At this point the female might like to take the remaining ████████ and carefully insert it into your ████████. By now you should be in a state of either extreme pleasure or excruciating agony. It's now time to take the █████████, remembering to wash it thoroughly beforehand, and ram it right up your partner's ████████. You may now █████ ████████ ██████ ████ ████████. Should at any point the ████████ become ████████ you should ████████ ███ ████████ ████████ ████████ ████████ ████████ ████████ ████████ ████████ ████████ ████████ ████████ ████████ █████████ and seek immediate medical advice.

11

STDs

The down side to sexual promiscuity is that unless you use protection you run the risk of contracting a sexually transmitted disease. STDs come in a wide variety with symptoms ranging from a slight rash to flames shooting out the end of your dick. Recent years have seen a steady increase in cases of nob-rot and this can be attributed to two basic factors, the first of which is ignorance.

A recent survey carried out in Scotland revealed an astonishing level of ignorance concerning sexually transmitted diseases. Of 5,000 males aged 18-40 who were surveyed, 18% thought that STD was the button between BBC2 and Channel 4 on the telly, 21% thought that Herpes was one of the Marx Brothers, 37% thought that Syphilis was a Greek island, 49% thought that Chlamydia was Prince Charles's wife and a staggering 65% thought that Gonorrhoea was an Italian centre forward who used to play for Hibernian in the early nineties.

"We have your test results back, Mr Tait, and I'm afraid it's worse than we first anticipated."

The second factor in the increase of STDs is down to condom manufacturers who, in a devilishly clever marketing ploy, introduced a line of sheaths specifically designed for the slightly more well endowed gentleman. This in turn meant that sexually responsible hoor maisters who popped into Boots for their weekly pack of three, were being given a choice of sizes. Taking the fragile male ego into account, it doesn't take a genius to realise that there weren't too many who opted for the small ones.

If you suspect that you might have caught a dose, you should immediately make an appointment with your local STD clinic. Don't be put off by stories you may have heard concerning the treatment of venereal disease. Times have changed since the days when it took two burly nurses to hold you down while a doctor inserted a white hot needle resembling a golf umbrella up your hog's eye. This is the 21st century after all, and they now use a chair with thick restraining straps.

There is still a stigma surrounding STDs and some guys are put off by the idea of visiting a clinic because they feel embarrassed and are worried that the doctors and nurses will make fun of them. Nothing could be further from the truth and you will find the staff sympathetic and discreet. That is, of course, until you have left the premises, when they will laugh mercilessly at your misfortune and post photographs of your festering boaby on the internet.

Should you find yourself in the unenviable position of having to wait a couple of weeks for test results, it's best to curtail your sexual activity during this period and try not to worry yourself too much. Take solace in the case of the 22-year-old Dundonian man who discovered his penis had turned yellow and was giving off a pungent aroma of cheese. Following weeks of tests at his local STD clinic, all of which came back negative, the cause of his condition was eventually put down to his habit of eating Quavers while watching the Adult Channel.

The worst case scenario would be for you to contract HAGS. This is an all-new hybrid virus which contains elements of herpes, AIDS, gonorrhoea and syphilis. Should you find yourself being diagnosed with HAGS you will immediately be admitted to hospital and put on a strict diet of Jacob's cream crackers and After Eight mints. This will not cure you but it's the only thing they'll be able to slide under the fucking door.

AFTERWORD

All that now remains is to equip yourself with the most important item in the hoor maister's arsenal. You will need to find yourself a piece of wood approximately twenty-four to thirty inches in length and no more than one and a half inches in diameter. You can purchase this from your local timber merchant, although a branch from a tree would serve just as well.

Take a roll of electrical tape and wind it around one end so that it covers approximately six inches of the stick. This is the handle. Now take your stick to wherever thoughtless dog owners take their overfed canines to empty their guts. A children's play park or the pavement outside a shoe shop should suffice. Now, using an old rubber glove, smear a generous amount of dog shit all over the remaining length of the stick and allow to dry.

Ideally, you should get into the habit of carrying this most vital piece of equipment with you at all times because, from here on, with the information you now possess, you will almost certainly find that you have to beat the girls off with a shitty stick.